NATURE   SERIES

WILD FLOWERS

By
JACQUELINE SEYMOUR

Designed by
DAVID GIBBON

Produced by
TED SMART

COLOUR LIBRARY INTERNATIONAL

INTRODUCTION

The course of evolution has shown that those individuals or species which are the most adaptable to changing circumstances are the most successful in the struggle for survival. This flexibility is achieved by sexual reproduction which, for somewhat complicated genetic reasons, produces variations, some of which will either be improvements on the original or be better able to respond to changing conditions. The flower is the plant's way of achieving such sexual interchange.

Flowering plants include grasses, herbaceous plants, shrubs and trees. The flowers of grasses are small and inconspicuous as are those of many trees. They produce large quantities of pollen which is scattered by the wind, so coming into contact with the female part of the flower and fusing to form, eventually, a seed. This is rather a hit-and-miss affair and other flowering plants, those we shall

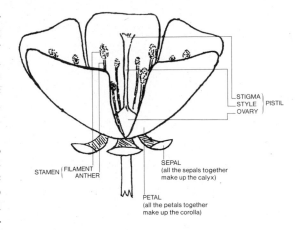

consider in this book, have evolved more elaborate, precise and less wasteful methods. The flower is designed to attract a pollinator. Indeed some plants are so specialised that only one species of insect is capable of achieving pollination. Others have a more general structure and different members of the animal world can pollinate them, and some pollinate themselves. (This last method is often a second best. Some seeds, even if they do not produce the range of variations that would have occurred had the pollen come from a different plant, are better than none at all.) Besides providing a suitable landing platform, attractants to the plant include colour, scent and nectar. Insect visitors collect nectar and pollen. Other visitors are bats and birds. The structure of the flower obviously varies to accommodate these different animals and methods. A diagram of a generalised simple flower is shown here with the main parts labelled. The parts of the flower are referred to from time to time in the text but the Glossary on page 63 explains these and other botanical terms used.

It is not possible to consider the flower in isolation. Obviously it is intimately connected with the rest of the plant, the form of which in turn depends a great deal on the conditions in which it is growing. Botanists usually distinguish three main types of vegetation; desert, forest and grassland. Desert plants live in the most hostile environment of all suffering intense heat, extreme cold and, most significant of all, drought. Tropical forest plants have the problems of heat and heavy rainfall. Plants of grasslands, having less extreme conditions, are not so highly specialised. Tropical plants can frequently adapt to more temperate climates but the process is not so successful the other way round. In extreme conditions plants tend to be evergreen and the leaves are partially protected by a thick cuticle from the dangers of desiccation. In hot climates the plants are large and flowers are often very gaudy. In the arctic the plants are small so as little as possible is exposed to the elements, the habit being characteristically a rosette, mat or hummock, or if a shrub then often a creeping plant. They often have very strong far-reaching roots which perform the dual function of collecting water and holding the plant safely in the soil. The compactness reduces water loss, but other adaptations arise which also do this. Leaves develop waxy or leathery coatings or become covered in hairs which insulate and reduce water loss by keeping a layer of still air next to the plant. In some cases succulence reduces the ratio between the water-holding capacity and the leaf area, although this adaptation is best seen in the desert plants, particularly cacti. Arctic plants are adapted to a very short flowering season, some blooming, fruiting and dying in about six weeks.

On a smaller scale than the examples just cited the same species can appear very different in form when growing in different habitats. A plant clinging to a pocket of earth on a rocky ledge two thousand metres up a mountain may appear small and stunted beside its brother in the valley below. If the two are grown under identical conditions it will become obvious that they are in fact the same species. This brings up the problem of classification of plants, which, albeit at a fairly superficial level, is unavoidable when discussing them. English names are not standardised and vary greatly from region to region. The Latin system is understood and used by botanists all over the world. A family is a group of plants in which certain characteristics are constant. This usually refers to the shape of the flower, which is after all the most obvious starting point when trying to establish interrelationships. The family is the main division used in the book–for example the next two pages show members of the Buttercup family. A family is divided into genera (the singular is genus) which are subgroups indicating a putative common ancestor. Members of a genus are called species. The definition of a species is a knotty problem but the main considerations in the plant world are structural ones–the members all appear to be the same.

Wild flowers have provided the ancestors of all our ornamental and food plants. Some of these varieties have arisen spontaneously, many more have been deliberately bred, often utilising the property that many species hybridise very easily. For the purpose of this book wild flowers are those which have arisen without man's conscious interference, and are simply the result of many millions of years of evolution.

Left : Meadow wild flowers including Campanulas and Buttercups

The Buttercup family (Ranunculaceae) is considered by many botanists to be one of the most primitive among the flowering plants. Some of the earliest fossil pollen discovered belongs to this group. The flowers are of the simple type illustrated on the previous page, with sepals, petals, stamens and pistils separate from each other. In some cases there are no petals and the sepals are coloured like petals as in the Pasque Flower *left*. In this picture the long purple stigmas can be seen surrounded by the anthers. The stigmas ripen first and so are receptive to pollen from other individuals before the pollen in the same flower is shed. This ensures favourable conditions for cross-pollination. Bees are the main pollinators but beetles, bugs and thrips visit the flower. The outer anthers do not produce pollen but are modified to form nectaries. As the flower matures pollen becomes available for collection as well as nectar. Self-pollination can then occur if cross-fertilisation has not already taken place.

Besides possessing a simple flower structure another primitive feature is that many species of the family grow in damp or marshy places. Nevertheless there are still others which display characteristics generally considered to be much more specialised, both in their vegetative growth and in their ecological distribution; there are, for example, alpine and arctic types.

The Meadow Buttercup seen growing in an English meadow *below* is a typical member of the *Ranunculus* genus. *Ranunculus* means "little frog" and refers to the fact that many species grow in moist places. The plant is also called Meadow Crowfoot and is one of several species known as Bachelor's Buttons. Meadow Buttercups have a wide distribution being found from Greenland and Spain eastwards to China and Japan. Their floral arrangement and development is similar to that of the Pasque Flower although they possess both sepals and petals. Nectar is secreted beneath a small flap-like scale at the base of each petal, but in this case the pollen is self-incompatible and seeds will not form unless pollen from another plant is deposited on the stigmas. Bees and flies are the most common insects that do this.

Buttercups (i.e. *Ranunculus* sp.) have five sepals and five petals which are coloured white, red or yellow. The leaves are typically divided and have a general resemblance to birds' feet, giving rise to the other common name of Crowfoot. The Mount Cook Lily *bottom right* is a buttercup which grows in the Southern Alps of New Zealand. It has adapted to a less favourable environment, flourishing on stony soil up to 1500m. The leaves are partly protected against water loss by the glossy covering, but as the plant grows in the shade they are large to allow it to obtain enough light for photosynthesis.

Aquilegia or Columbine flowers have a more complicated structure. They have five coloured sepals between which the concave petals project back into long spurs each containing a separate nectary. The Blue Columbine *top right* is found in the western United States, but there are also white, violet, pink and red forms. The red ones also occur in the United States where they are pollinated by humming birds, their long beaks enabling them to reach into the spur in their search for nectar. Similarly, hawk moths visit the white ones. Pollination can also be effected by those who are collecting pollen alone although they may not possess the sort of mouth parts that would allow access to the nectar.

There are about four hundred species in the Poppy family. A well known member is the Opium Poppy, a close relative of the Corn or Field Poppy *right*. The flowers of the Corn Poppy open in the early morning and last for only one day.

The Pale Corydalis *top left* is related to the poppies and is found in the east and central United States. Corydalis is the Greek name for the crested lark and the flower is so called because a single spur of the four-petalled corolla is twisted above the rest of the flower to form a crest.

Sacred or Indian Lotuses, growing on Lake Dal, Srinagar, Kashmir *below*, belong to the water lily family. This is not the lotus of the Egyptians or the ancient lotus-eaters, but the plant is remarkable in that the seeds remain capable of germination for hundreds of years after they are shed.

The Mustard family (Cruciferae) consists of plants found mainly in mild regions and includes a number of the weed plants of Europe, Asia and North America. The wild flowers include shepherd's purse, penny-cress, bitter-cress, the rockets, pepperwort and the Cuckoo Flower, Milkmaids or Lady's Smock *left*. The Lady's Smock has very attractive flowers which by a stretch of the imagination can be seen to be like little smocks hanging out to dry. Cultivated members of this family include the flowers sweet alyssum, candytuft, honesty, stock and wall-flower and the vegetables cabbage, cauliflower, kale, radish and turnip.

Cistuses are a family of shrubs found mainly in the Mediterranean region. They are also known as Rock-roses although they are not related to the Rose family. The Gum Cistus *below* was photographed in Spain. It, with some other Cistus species, is the source of a resinous gum called ladanum which is used in perfumes and for fumigation. The gum is secreted by glands on the sticky shoots and leaves. It is collected by pulling strips of cloth or leather through the bushes and also by combing the beards of goats who have been browsing on the dry hillsides where the shrubs are found.

The violet has come to be a symbol of innocence and modesty but it was believed by the ancients to have sprung from the blood of the boaster Ajax. The wild Pansy or Heartsease is an ancestor of the many beautiful cultivated pansies which have been so successfully developed partly because violets hybridise so easily. This property makes identifying wild violets rather difficult because it results in the appearance of intermediate forms. The Heath Dog Violet *above* shows the five typical unequal free petals. Nectar collects in the lowest petal which is extended at the base to form a spur. It attracts bees and hoverflies.

Cleomes are members of the Caper family and are found in the tropics and warm temperate regions. The one on the right is an African species and the picture shows the typically long exaggerated stamens. This genus is often pollinated by bats; the stamens brushing pollen over their bodies as they visit the flowers for nectar.

The Pink family (Caryophyllaceae) is typically found in milder regions of the northern hemisphere.

The stamens of the Greater Stitchwort *top left* are arranged in two rings of five. The outer ones ripen first, then bend towards the middle of the flower and shed their pollen. They then bend towards their original position and are replaced by the inner ones.

Spurreys are adapted to soils rich in salt. The Cliff Spurrey or Cliff Sandspurrey *below* is found on coastal cliffs, rocks and walls in western Europe.

The Cushion Pink or Moss Campion *top right* is another plant adapted to a rather inhospitable environment. It is an arctic-alpine species, found mainly in North America and Europe, which grows in a dense low mat typical of such plants.

The larger tubular flowers of the Red Campion *bottom right* are unisexual. Male and female flowers are borne on different plants so the Red Campion is totally dependent on cross pollination for its survival. It is visited by bees and long-tongued flies.

11

The most famous member of the Mallow family (Malvaceae) is the cotton plant. The hollyhock, flowering maple and rose-mallow or hibiscus are others. The Musk Mallow *left* is a native of Europe which has spread and become naturalised so that it is quite common in North America. It is a perennial with rose-pink (or occasionally white) petals found in fields and hedgerows.

The appearance of plants in places foreign to them is usually directly related to man's activities. As transport has increased so has the intentional and unintentional importation of aliens. Many of these introductions are unable to compete with the well-adapted native forms, but many others have become strikingly successful. These grow in waste places and on roadsides, often being first found at ports, alongside railways and at rubbish dumps. Such weeds are characterised by a marked lack of specialisation, adapting to a range of soil types, rainfall, temperature and day length. Paradoxically, in view of what has already been said about the value of sexual reproduction, most of the successful weeds are self-pollinated. This does in fact confer an advantage on these plants, and partly explains their success. Many of them are annuals; annuals which self-fertilise are capable of recovering from a bad year and are not dependent on insects who too may suffer from bad conditions. Moreover, if self-fertile, a single specimen can give rise to a whole new population.

Two members of the Purslane family are shown on the right. The Carolina Spring Beauty *above* is now considered to be a different genus *(Claytonia)* from the Spring Beauty *(Montia perfoliata) below*. The first genus was named after Dr. John Clayton, an 18th century American botanist. The small white flowers have delicate pink veins and appear in rich woods in North America in spring. The *Montia* genus was named after another 18th century botanist, the professor of botany at Bologna, Guiseppe Monti. *Montia perfoliata* was so called because the flowering stem appears to perforate a circular leaf. This is in fact two leaves which have become united, but the form has given rise to the delightful name of Button-hole Plant. This picture shows the small white flowers with the three-cleft styles rising above the five stamens which are opposite the petals and attached to their bases.

There is an old-fashioned saying "when the gorse is out of bloom, kissing is out of fashion" which is a charming way of expressing the fact that Gorse *left* can be found in flower all the year round. The flowers are nectarless but insects visit to collect pollen, probably attracted by the strong coconut-like smell. When a bee enters the flower the keel petals (see page 16 for a description of the structure of a flower) break apart and the stamens and style are brought sharply into contact with the abdomen of the insect so depositing and receiving pollen respectively. The central flower in the picture has been exploded in this way. Once exploded a flower is rarely visited again. The seed pods which subsequently develop gradually dry out as the seeds ripen until suddenly the two sides of the pod split apart and curl up spirally, so scattering the seeds.

Gorse is a member of the Pea family (Leguminosae) as is the Kaka Beak or Parrot Bill *below* which is a Glory-pea found only on the North Island of New Zealand. It is so called because of its resemblance to the bill of the Kaka, a New Zealand parrot.

In common with most other tropical plants tropical members of the Pea family have much larger flowers than those in more temperate climates. It follows therefore that the seed pods are also larger and the sounds made by the explosive mechanism of seed dispersal have been likened to a fusillade of gun shots. D'Alberti's Creeper *above* is a tropical creeper found in New Guinea. Like other members of its genus *(Mucuna)* it is bat-pollinated. Tropical climbers are known as lianas and compete successfully with the vast tropical trees in their quest for adequate light. In doing so they have become some of the longest plants in the world; a length of over two hundred metres has been recorded.

Erythrinas are found throughout the tropics. Coloured red and orange but lacking scent they are bird-pollinated. *Erythrina humeana, right,* was photographed in Transkei, South Africa. Larger species form a scrub which is ecologically important because it is fire resistant, an adaptation to regular bush fires.

A typical pea plant climbs by means of its tendrils, has compound leaves, irregular butterfly-like flowers and bears its seeds in pods. The five petals of the corolla are unequal in size and shape. The uppermost one is large and conspicuous, the lateral ones smaller with narrow bases and the two lower ones joined to form an upturned keel.

Few families of flowering plants have more members than the pea family and few families have produced as many species useful to man, who cultivates them as ornamental and food plants. These include lupins, vetches, wistaria, alfalfa, clover, peas, beans and the peanut. Lupins *top left* grow wild in North America, forming beautiful patches of colour rather like Bluebells *(Endymion)* do in England, sometimes looking like a blue carpet. The name Lupin is derived from the Latin word for wolf *(lupus)* indicating that they were thought to impoverish the soil. On the contrary, legumes assist in the survival of all vegetation, both wild and cultivated. Nitrogen is necessary for the growth of all animals and plants but they are unable to utilise it directly from the air, where it is available in plenty. A bacterium called *Rhizobium* forms nodules in the roots of some legumes and this symbiotic association achieves nitrogen fixation. Without this mechanism the nitrogen in the soil would now be so depleted that the present amount of vegetation in the world could not possibly exist.

Two coastal species of the genus *Caesalpinia* are remarkable because they bear seeds which will float for many years without losing the power of germination, like the seeds of the Indian Lotus. The Bird of Paradise Flower *bottom left* is also a *Caesalpinia* but it grows inland. It is shown here in Arizona.

Sweet peas are among the most popular plants for producing cut flowers. The Earth-nut Pea *right* is a close relative which grows in parts of Europe.

The Dog Rose *top left* is the most common and the largest of the wild roses found in Britain. There are more than one hundred species of wild rose and all our cultivated roses have been developed from these forms. The rose family has provided man with a large number of useful species including the strawberry, raspberry and blackberry and most of the common fruit trees (apple, pear, cherry etc.).

The remaining pictures on these two pages show members of the Willow-herb or Evening Primrose family (Onagraceae). Fuchsias are native to Central and South America and are shown here *bottom left* in Argentina. The tubular flowers have coloured sepals which are usually red, the corolla being purple. The flowers are bird-pollinated. Cultivated Fuchsias display a variety of different shapes and colours.

Evening Primroses are native to North America and are typically found in dry, open habitats. The Yellow Evening Primrose *top right* is shown in just such a place, the White Sands National Monument in New Mexico. Some species of Evening Primrose open only at night, which explains their name. The large pale flowers attract night-flying moths. The flowers of Rosebay Willow-herb or Fireweed *bottom right* are as beautiful as those of many cultivated plants, but the plant has the undesirable characteristic of spreading extremely rapidly which makes it unsatisfactory as a garden flower. Common in North America, Europe and Asia, it is shown here growing on the Alaskan tundra. In good conditions in more temperate areas it can reach a height of two metres. It has become noted for its sudden appearance on London bomb sites in the Second World War. This tendency to grow on ground which has been burnt may be responsible for the name "Fireweed"; alternatively the name may refer to the resemblance of the massed plants to a blazing fire. The Rosebay Willow-herb is well adapted for cross-pollination. Bees visit flowers at the bottom of the spike first. These flowers are the most mature, producing nectar and being ready for pollination. Pollen from another plant is therefore deposited by the bee collecting nectar, which, as it climbs higher up the spike, also collects pollen. It flies on to the bottom of the next spike and the process is repeated.

Examples of red flowers shown in this book are often accompanied by the information that the flower is bird- or bat-pollinated. This colour has been shown to be particularly attractive to these two groups of animals as it is to day-flying butterflies. Bees are also visitors to red or reddish flowers like the Corn Poppy or Rosebay Willowherb, which seems odd in the light of the fact that bees are red-blind. Karl von Frisch performed some famous and fascinating experiments in which he demonstrated that bees could not distinguish between red, black and dark grey. Bees can, however, detect rays from the ultraviolet end of the spectrum that man is not sensitive to. This explains why they are attracted to certain red flowers; these flowers are the ones which reflect ultraviolet light. Bees are also unable to discriminate between yellow-orange and yellow-green, so their colour sense is in any case less well developed than our own. But their sensitivity to ultraviolet light means that many other flowers appear differently to them as well; to a bee, for example, daisies look bluish-green.

This demonstrates how precisely flowers have become adapted to attract what is presumably the most efficient pollinator. Humming-bird red is not the same as bee red, which in its turn is different from butterfly red.

Most of the members of the Myrtle family are native to Australia and the American tropics. They are often shrubs or trees, like the Eucalyptus or Gum Trees, with evergreen aromatic leaves and showy flowers. The Stirling Range Bell *left* is a heather-like Australian plant belonging to this family. The tiny true flowers are completely hidden by large coloured bracts.

The Red or Green Kangaroo-paw *right* is another plant (family Haemodoraceae) found only in Australia. It is the state flower of Western Australia. The flower has a very odd form. The stems and base of the flower tube are red and the pale green segments of the flower are bent back showing the six large protruding stamens. This Kangaroo-paw flowers in the spring and is found in a variety of habitats including sand plains and forest.

All the members of the Four O'Clock family (Nyctaginaceae) have flowers which lack petals. This does not mean to say that they are dull or inconspicuous. Many have coloured sepals and/or bracts like the Bougainvillea *below*, a native of tropical America which has been introduced throughout the tropics.

Proteas are a large southern family found on all the continents south of the equator. This group is best known for its representatives in South Africa and Australia, where the greatest concentration of species can be found. Proteas carry many small flowers in a 'cup' of tightly fitting bracts. They produce a profuse amount of nectar and are normally bird pollinated. The sugarbirds of southern Africa breed in Protea vegetation and time their breeding activities to coincide with the nectar flow. They also use fluff from the inflorescences to line their nests. The King Protea *below* is the most dramatic and showy of the African Proteas.

Australian Proteas like the Scarlet Banksia *left* and the Gippsland Waratah *right* are pollinated by birds called honey-eaters. The dense spikes of the *Banksia* inflorescence open from the bottom upwards and can bear as many as one thousand flowers.

The Passion Flower *left* was given its name by early missionaries to tropical America, where the four hundred species occur, because they saw in it a resemblance to the instruments of the Passion. The leaf symbolised the spear, the five anthers the five wounds received by Christ on the cross. The nails themselves were represented by the triple style, the fleshy threads within the flower suggested the crown of thorns, and so on. What is more the flower is supposed to remain open for three days, symbolising the three years of Christ's ministry. The plant is a climber; tendrils arising from the stem grow cork-screw fashion around anything they touch. Passion Flowers are cultivated and prized for their beautiful colours and extravagant shape.

Another tropical plant which has become widely cultivated is the Begonia *below*. The attractively coloured leaves and ease of propagation has made Begonias particularly popular for this purpose.

Rather than being noted for beautiful flowers, the members of the Gourd family (Cucurbitaceae) are known for their large and peculiar fruits which include pumpkins, melons and cucumbers. The Squirting Cucumber *above* is one of the few representatives of the family which is found growing wild in Europe. It grows as a weed throughout the Mediterranean region. When the fruit ripens it becomes detached from the stalk, either as a result of its own weight or after a jolt from a passing animal, with an effect rather like a cork popping out of a bottle of champagne. The release in pressure shoots out the seeds inside a jet of pungent liquid which can travel several metres.

Purple Loosestrife *right* is another European representative of a family (Lythraceae) which has few other species growing in the area. It is also found in Asia, Africa and America. Loosestrifes are found throughout the world except for cold regions, but most grow in the American tropics. Their flowers are typically purplish; yellow flowers called loosestrife belong to the primrose family.

Cacti are found growing wild only in America, especially in the western United States. Their shapes have evolved as a solution to the problem of survival in extremely inhospitable conditions. They can survive extreme heat, lack of water and some are adapted to a cold night temperature, being found high in the Andes. Any plant in a hot dry climate has the dual problem of water loss and water conservation. Leaves are large areas of chlorophyll-containing cells which carry out the process of photosynthesis. Large thin areas like this lose a lot of water to the atmosphere by evaporation. This is unimportant where plenty of water is available but in dryish conditions methods have evolved to reduce this loss; one of the most common is the development of a thick waxy cuticle. In tropical regions where there is plenty of sun the amount of leaf area is relatively unimportant, so in addition this is often much reduced. Cacti demonstrate this process carried to its logical conclusion. They have dispensed with leaves altogether; all that remain of them are spines. The stems contain chlorophyll and are much enlarged, forming water stores. The minimum surface area for the maximum storage volume has been achieved by the stems, being un-branched cylinders or hemispherical in shape. Some species have enlarged tuberous roots which also store water; the roots of each extend an amazingly long way from the visible plant in their search for water.

Any plant growing where others cannot will inevitably be used by animals for food; the spines thus have a protective function but these are not totally effective as the plants are still attacked by birds and rodents. Some birds nest in the larger species, flickers and owls being found in the giant saguaros.

These weird and misshapen plants have exquisite flowers so that in the springtime the desert comes alive with beautiful colours. The Prickly Pear (Opuntia) genus is the largest of the family. A few species of this genus have become naturalised in other parts of the world becoming troublesome weeds. The flowers of the Purple-tinged Prickly Pear are shown *top left.*

The Barrel Cactus *bottom left* can be used as a source of drinking water by the traveller in the desert. The Hedgehog or Strawberry Cactus *top right* bears strawberry-like fruits. After the spines are brushed off they are as delicious to eat as strawberries. The virtually spherical Cory Cactus *bottom right* has achieved maximum storage volume with minimum water loss by adopting this shape.

Another group of plants which has adapted to adverse conditions by developing succulence, this time of the leaves, is the Stonecrop or Orpine family (Crassulaceae). This includes the Houseleeks, sixty species of which grow in mountainous parts of the world. This one *left* is the Mountain Houseleek, photographed in the Pyrenees. The name leek is derived from an Anglo-Saxon word that simply means plant, and houseleeks can often be seen growing on roofs. Indeed they were often deliberately planted there as a protection against witches and lightning. Stonecrops can also be found growing on roofs and walls. The attractive yellow flowers of a Stonecrop, the Wall-pepper, are shown *below*.

Saxifrages, too, often have thick leaves, although a separate family group, and are often found in rocky crevices. The generic name of the Meadow Saxifrage *right*, *Saxifraga*, means rock-breaker, although this particular species is found in grassland and not on rocks.

Most people are familiar with pictures of carnivorous or insectivorous plants even if they have not seen them growing. These pictures usually show the modified leaves with which the plant traps its prey, rather than the flowers shown here; the Venus Fly Trap *above* and the American Pitcher Plant *below*. Pitcher plants are also found in Australia and in the tropics but all three kinds have been placed in different families, indicating that they are believed to have evolved separately. There are ten species of *Sarracenia*, the American Pitcher Plant, which have such common names as Sidesaddle Flower, Devil's Boot, Frog Bonnet and Bog Bugle. The flowers are purple-red with five sepals and petals and the expanded top of the pistil forms a cap at the centre (i.e. the underside) of the flower. The leaves are green, attractively veined and tinged with red. They grow in a rosette at the base of the stem and each one is rolled lengthwise to form a long conical tube, open at the top. There are rows of hairs forming ridges inside the leaf and pointing downwards so that insects once in the trap, having been attracted by the smell of the viscous liquid produced by the plant, are unable to climb out. The pitchers collect rain water in which the insects drown and then decay, until the remains can be absorbed by special cells at the base.

The Venus Fly Trap is another North American species. Its leaves have adopted a different form, having semi-circular symmetrical lobes which lie almost flat. In the middle of each half of the leaf are three long spines or trigger hairs, and rigid bristle-like teeth coloured green and crimson fringe the edges. Tiny glands secrete a sticky liquid on to the leaf. These shiny colourful leaves are attractive to insects which, in landing, touch the trigger hairs, causing the trap to snap shut in less than a quarter of a minute. The teeth round the edge interlock making escape difficult. The plant secretes digestive juices which decompose the body before absorption. The length of this process varies from a week to a month depending on the size and nature of the prey. The Venus Fly Trap is a member of the Sundew family, which also includes the Butterworts. Butterworts, Sundews and the Venus Fly Trap share a common method of trapping their food; namely the leaves are capable of movement and secrete digestive juices. All these plants, however, contain chlorophyll and so carry out the more conventional process of photosynthesis as well as their carnivorous activities.

The inflorescences of plants belonging to the Carrot or Parsley family (Umbellifereae) are umbrella shaped. The individual flowers are tiny with five sepals and five petals and are grouped together to form partial umbels. These partial umbels are in turn grouped to form a big umbel. This structure can be seen in the picture of Giant Hogweed *right*. This plant grows to an enormous size and in favourable conditions can reach a height of four metres. The umbels measure up to half a metre across. It is a native of the Caucasus but can be found growing wild in many parts of Europe. The Cow Parsley shown growing on an English cart track *below* is the first of this family to appear here in early summer. It is sometimes called Queen Anne's Lace, a name which is also given to the wild carrot. Because their tiny flowerheads are concentrated in a cluster of this kind these plants display a mass of attractive colour; this, together with the flat shape, attracts a variety of insects.

The Daisy family (Compositae) contains more genera than any other family of flowering plants and has many representatives in all parts of the world. It is therefore surprising to learn that little use is made of it agriculturally compared with, for example, the Pea and Rose families which have far fewer species.

The Stemless Carline Thistle *top left* is adapted to grow in mountainous districts and is found in Europe in poor meadows, on rocky slopes and in open woods. It is a perennial, the rosette growing flat on the ground. The flower is surrounded by attractive silver bracts. It is sometimes dried and used as a weather glass—the bracts close together in damp air. The roots are used in herbal remedies. The name Carline Thistle is supposed to have arisen because the Emperor Charlemagne, praying for help when his men were dying of disease, had his prayers answered by an angel, who fired an arrow after telling him that the plant it fell on, a thistle, would cure the disease.

The Spear Thistle *bottom left* is one of a genus of about one hundred and twenty species found in the northern hemisphere. All are pervasive weeds which spread rapidly by means of their silky-haired seeds known as thistle-down. Native to Europe, Africa and west Asia, the Spear Thistle has been introduced to North America and China. Found in fields, roadsides and waste places, it is visited by long-tongued bees, hoverflies and butterflies.

Hawkweeds are what is known as apomitic, as are dandelions. This means that they produce seed without pollination i.e. asexually. They are efficient propagators with a huge seed production. There are about three hundred species of Hawkweed. The Orange Hawkweed *far right* is a native of central Europe but is now found all over Europe and in North America. It has a number of common names, including Dirty Dick, Grim the Collier and Devil's Paintbrush.

The Black-eyed Susan or Yellow Cone Flower *near right* is a well-known plant of the North American plains. It has orange-yellow ray flowers and a central cone of purplish-brown disc flowers.

Didelta carnosa, below right, is a South African Daisy, seen here flowering in sand dunes near Table View in the South West Cape.

The umbels shown on the previous page are examples of flowers becoming clustered together and so achieving greater efficiency. The typical composite flower head is the climax of the evolution of efficient flower clusters. It

is often mistaken for an individual flower, particularly as the central flowers are often coloured yellow like stamens. These central or disc flowers are fertile and produce stamens and pistils but the outer or ray flowers are modified to attract insects and are sterile. Bracts which occur at the bases of the individual flower stalks form an involucre beneath the head of flowers. This is frequently mistaken for a calyx but in a typical composite the calyx is not green and leaf-like but is modified into scales, bristles or down which are often instrumental in ensuring the dispersal of the seeds.

The Silversword *left* is a dramatic and unusual annual found growing only on the islands of Hawaii and Maui. It grows from 1500 to 3660 metres in volcanic ash and cinders and is shown here in the crater of Haleakala volcano. It has been the victim of exploitation in the past, being dried for ornaments and sent to east Asia at the beginning of the century. It is also vulnerable to attack by insect larvae which destroy the seed, particularly vital to any annual plant. The Silversword has an extreme habitat. It grows at a high altitude where it is warm in the daytime and very cold at night and the air is excessively dry. The rosette of leaves protected by masses of woolly hairs is obviously adapted to these adverse conditions. The stem is enormous, growing to a diameter of about sixty centimetres before the inflorescence develops. This in turn can rise to a height of over one and half metres. There are more hairs on the upper part of the stalk and on the inflorescence but these are glandular and produce a sticky secretion which is thought to prevent crawling insects from pollinating the flowers, so encouraging cross-pollination.

The Feverfew *top right* is a more familiar plant which was probably native to south-east Europe, Asia Minor and the Caucasus but which is now common in all parts of Europe and south-east Asia. It has a stongly aromatic smell and was formerly cultivated as a medicinal plant, being used to reduce fever, hence the name. It was also used as an insecticide and has similar properties to pyrethrum, which is a powder extracted from the flowerheads of another *Chrysanthemum* species. The wedge-shaped ray florets of the Feverfew are white, the disc florets are yellow, as are those of *Celmisia coriacea, centre right,* a characteristic species of New Zealand. The flowering heads measure about ten centimetres across and the leaves are leathery and hairy. Ursinias *bottom right* are orange daisies found in South Africa.

Members of the Heath family (Ericaceae) are found in arctic and temperate regions and on mountains in the tropics. They are largely trees and shrubs and include azaleas and rhododendrons. There are very few species in Australia. The genus *Erica* is common through much of Europe and tropical Africa but the highest concentration of species is found in southern Africa where *Erica vestita, left,* comes from.

Blueberry pie is a well-known American dish. Some blueberries are specially cultivated but most of the market supply in the United States comes from wild plants. Bilberries, Blueberries, Whortleberries, Huckleberries, Cranberries and Cowberries all come from members of the genus *Vaccinum*–indeed the first four are all common names for the species *V. myrtilus*. *Vaccinum* species are shrubs with white or pink flowers *top right*.

The Trailing Arbutus or Mayflower *bottom right* grows in North America. Tradition has it that it was named the Mayflower by the Pilgrim Fathers who saw it when they landed in the *Mayflower* at Plymouth, Massachusetts. It is extremely sensitive to environmental changes like lumbering and grazing. It is almost impossible to pick without uprooting and the desire of gardeners to have this charming flower growing on their own land is usually frustrated by the extreme difficulty of cultivation. The result is that it is endangered partly because it is so beautiful.

The nature of any vegetational community slowly changes with the passage of time. The silting up of a lake is a clear-cut if rather extreme example of the way a habitat changes. Water flowing into a lake takes sediment with it; the result is that the lake will gradually silt up and become a marsh, with typical marsh plants. This too will dry out in the course of time and become a meadow, unsuitable for water-loving plants, and yet another plant community will develop. This type of vegetational succession is taking place in nearly all habitats, although obviously it is a process spread over hundreds or thousands of years.

Man's acquisitiveness and his destructiveness have a profound and rapid effect on plant communities. He burns, excavates and builds; he grazes his animals and cultivates the soil intensively. The resilience of members of the plant kingdom is remarkable and plants continue to appear in many apparently unfavourable circumstances, but inevitably many of the more delicate and specialised kinds will be lost if not deliberately preserved.

The Primrose family (Primulaceae) contains about four hundred species of herbaceous plants found in the northern hemisphere. Both the plants on this page belong to the *Primula* genus, the Primrose *left* and the Cowslip *below*. The name *Primula* refers to the early flowering of these species, coming from the word *primus* meaning first.

There are two well-known forms of Primrose, the pin eyed and the thrum eyed, which are found in wild populations in roughly equal proportions. In pins the style is long so that it is seen at the opening of the corolla, as in the picture, with the stamens hidden half way down the corolla tube. In the thrum flower the position of anthers and stigma are reversed. The possible significance of this was realised by Charles Darwin when he observed that primroses and cowslips did not seed if insects were prevented from visiting them and he concluded that this was an evolutionary mechanism preventing self-fertilisation. Insects that visit the flowers have long proboscises with which they search for nectar. Pollen collects on the proboscis at different levels depending on whether the flower is a pin or a thrum, and is therefore placed at the optimum position for pollinating the other type of flower when the insect moves on.

Gentians occur in alpine and temperate parts of the world. Their tubular or trumpet-shaped flowers are normally blue in Europe, Asia and North America, but red Gentians grow in South America and those of New Zealand are white. The long-stalked Fringed Gentian *right* grows in meadows and damp woods in the northern United States and southern Canada. The four delicately fringed petals that give the flower its name can be clearly seen in the photograph. This is quite a large flower that grows up to five centimetres in length. The smaller but vividly coloured Spring Gentian *below* grows in the mountains of central Europe.

Gentians have been used medicinally for hundreds of years. An infusion made from the juicy root of the yellow gentian is used in Europe for digestive disturbances. This root often grows to the thickness of an arm as the plant lives for over fifty years. The roots of Gentians have a bitter taste so that both cattle and rodents refuse to eat them.

. The Gentian family also includes the marsh pinks and the centauries.

The Alpine Forget-me-not *left* and Chiming Bells *below, far left* are both members of the Borage family and were photographed in Alaska. This Forget-me-not is the floral emblem of Alaska. The Chiming Bells *(Mertensia)* are also known as Bluebells. This is a good example of the confusion that can be caused by using vernacular names. To the Englishman a Bluebell is a spring flower of the Lily family (genus *Endymion*) also known as the Wood-hyacinth; to the Scotsman it is a *Campanula* and to the North American Bluebell can mean a *Campanula*, or, as we see here, a species of *Mertensia*. To add to the confusion another member of the *Mertensia* genus is called a Cowslip. The European Cowslip is a *Primula*.

Bats-in-the-belfry *right* is also a bell-flower but it is a member of the Campanula family and found mainly in Europe.

Petrea, below, near left is a genus of the Verbena or Vervain family from tropical America. It contains about thirty species of trees, shrubs and woody vines.

The Cardinal Flower *left* is a *Lobelia* and is as evocative of the United States as the blueberry; in the same way primroses and bluebells bring thoughts of spring in England. The Cardinal Flower was one of the first American plants to be shipped to Europe for cultivation and has become well-known for this reason.

The Sky Pilot *right* belongs to the genus *Polemonium* which is a member of the Phlox family (Polemoniaceae). Most of the fifty species are found in North America, the Sky Pilot on tundra in the Rocky Mountains.

Honeysuckle *below* has pale flowers which open in the evening and release a sweet scent so attracting night-flying moths to which the long-tubed flowers are well adapted. The Honeysuckle family includes the elder, snowberry, guelder-rose and wayfaring-tree.

The Slender or Creeping Speedwell *left* is interesting because it rarely develops any seeds and yet it is phenomenally successful. It is native to the Caucasus where it is not common but it is now found all over Britain and is spreading in Europe and North America.

Like the Speedwells, Penstemons or Beardtongues are members of the Figwort family (Scrophulariaceae). They are strongly scented erect plants like the Azure Penstemon *right*. One of the stamens has become modified so that it is sterile, being flattened and bearded at the end, which protrudes from the flower like a tongue.

The Mint family are typically aromatic square-stemmed herbs and shrubs like the Lavender *below* which grows on warm stony hillsides like this one in Spain, and is widely cultivated for perfume. The flowers have scentless petals: the scent comes from the leaves and stem.

Representatives of three different families are shown on these two pages. They have in common their adaptations to life in dry conditions and illustrate African examples of evolution parallel to that of the American cacti – unrelated plants have found similar solutions to the problem of survival in hot arid regions. The Desert Rose *top left* is a member of the Dogbane family, Apocynaceae. The swollen stems serve as water reservoirs. The family has about one thousand members, mostly tropical shrubs, herbs and vines and includes oleanders and periwinkles. The plants characteristically have a milky juice.

Hoodia gordonii, bottom left, is a stapeliad, a member of the Asclepiadaceae. This succulent plant is typical of many stapeliads in mimicking the smell and appearance of decaying matter which attracts blow-flies and similar insects to it, so effecting pollination. Its leafless thorny appearance is obviously similar to that of many cacti as is the compressed glabrous growth of *Euphorbia breoni* from Madagascar *top right.*

There are more than one thousand species in the *Euphorbia* genus with a wide range of habit and habitat. There are succulents, trees, bushes and herbs but all have one thing in common, the structure of the inflorescence or cyathium, which is highly specialised. The flowers are very small, several male flowers being grouped round a single female flower in the cup-shaped cyathium. *Euphorbia robbiae, bottom right,* is a spurge from north west Asia Minor. The photograph shows the flowers close-up and also shows the four half-moon shaped glands which are nectarial bracts which attract insects.

Few members of the Euphorbia family have flowers which consist of a calyx and corolla. The majority lack a corolla; others lack both. Some of the flowers have coloured bracts or leaves which look like petals. They too have milky juice that is poisonous but which has been used successfully in the treatment of warts. Other members of the Euphorbia family include the Para rubber tree (the source of most of the world's rubber), the castor oil plant, tapioca plant and poinsettias.

The Bird of Paradise Flower *Strelitzia*, *above left*, from southern Africa and the *Heliconia* or wild plantain *right* from tropical America are both members of the Banana Family (Musaceae) and both flowers are of unusual construction. The Bird of Paradise Flower is bird-pollinated and several flowers arise out of each boat-shaped spathe in turn. This stout trough provides a platform for sugarbirds and sunbirds to alight on to extract nectar from the centre of the flower. Each flower consists of three outer orange segments and three inner blue segments. Two of these blue "petals" are united and enclose five thread-like anthers; the third is modified to form a nectar-producing pouch at the base. Like the Proteas the amount of nectar secreted is considerable. When the bird perches on the two fused petals to obtain the nectar the stamens are forced out of their sheath and come into contact with the underside of the bird, which then carries the pollen to the next plant it visits.

Heliconias too have boat-shaped spathes which are brightly coloured and which conceal a cluster of inconspicuous flowers. Lords-and-Ladies, Cuckoo Pint or Wild Arum *below left* is a native of Europe and North Africa and belongs to another family, the Aroids (Araceae) but it has a similar flower structure having a large spathe concealing a fleshy column bearing tiny flowers, the spadix. It has a remarkable pollination mechanism. The spadix bears female flowers in a zone at the base; above these are a few sterile flowers and above these in turn are the short-stalked stamens. The spathe opens about midday giving off a smell which is extremely attractive to insects, although, unlike many other Aroids which have particularly obnoxious scents, this is not particularly noticeable to man. During the afternoon and evening this smell is at its strongest and insects come to the plant deceived into believing that food awaits them. Instead they are trapped by the smooth surface and oily secretions of the plant, and if they have already visited another plant of the same species they pollinate the stigmas at the base of the spadix. The stigmas wither before the pollen is shed which it is in great quantity from the male parts of the spathe some hours later. The spadix withers and shrinks so allowing the pollen-covered insects to escape.

Other Aroids include the skunk cabbage, jack-in-the-pulpit, water lettuce and calla lilies.

The Meadow Saffron or Autumn Crocus *left* is a poisonous plant of damp meadows in Europe. It is not related to true *Crocus* species which belong to the Iris family, but is a member of the Lily family, as are all the flowers on the following five pages.

Maori Onions come from New Zealand. The species illustrated *below, Bulbinella rossii,* is the largest of them and is subantarctic being found on Auckland and Campbell Islands.

Red Hot Pokers *far right* have become popular garden flowers. They are seen here growing wild in south Africa.

The Glacier Lily *near right* is shown, appropriately enough, in Glacier National Park, Montana.

As already mentioned the name "Bluebell" refers to different flowers in different parts of the English-speaking world. The Bluebells shown here in close-up *bottom right* are the English Bluebell or Wood-hyacinth *(Endymion).*

51

Some members of the *Trillium* genus are native to eastern Asia but the genus is best known for its representatives in North America. The Large-flowered or White Trillium *left* is the floral emblem of Ontario. The name comes from the Latin word for three – the stem bears a whorl of three leaves and the flowers have three petals and three sepals.

There are a number of species of Solomon's Seal *below* all confined to northern temperate regions. The large tubular flowers are visited by long-tongued insects like bumble bees.

The Turk's Cap or Martagon Lily *right* really does look like oriental headgear. The flowers produce a strong scent at night attracting butterflies and moths, particularly the hummingbird hawkmoth. The perianth is specially adapted to the tongues of such insects, each part having its own nectar groove. If cross-pollination fails the flowers are capable of self-pollination.

The Peruvian Squill *left* seems oddly-named as it is a native of the Mediterranean. This photograph was taken in Spain. There are about eighty species of this genus, *Scilla,* found in temperate Eurasia and parts of Africa.

Flame or Glory Lilies are found in tropical Africa and Asia. They are atypical lilies because they can climb, having twining tendril tips to their leaves. *Gloriosa superba, below,* is shown growing in Namibia; the large brightly-coloured flowers are typical of the genus.

The Lily family is characterised by its underground stems and buds known as bulbs which give rise to clusters of grass-like leaves with parallel veins. The flowers are usually bell-like or triangular with the flower parts in threes. The segments of the perianth (i.e. sepals and petals) often look alike and are sometimes fused at the base to form a tubular, six-lobed corolla.

The *Allium* genus contains three hundred widely distributed species. They all have bulbs made up of a succession of overlapping layers of leaf-bases and white or pink flowers in umbrella-like clusters. The genus includes garlic and the leek, both of which are native to the Mediterranean, and also the common garden onion. The latter is no longer found in the wild state, having been cultivated for centuries. It was first used in India, Egypt and China and was grown throughout Europe even before the discovery of America. Ramsons *top right* is a member of the genus which produces white flowers in onion-like clusters. These contain partially-concealed nectar and are insect-pollinated. They are capable of self-pollination if cross-pollination fails. The plant grows in damp woods and shady places in much of Europe and Asia Minor and is unusual in that, because of a twist in the stalk, what is normally the underside of the leaf is turned upwards.

The Snakes-head Fritillary *bottom right* is also found in Europe. The shape of the flower-bud is like that of a snake's head and the name Fritillary comes from the Latin *fritillus* meaning a dice box. The name thus likens the markings on the petals to the markings on a chequerboard. The style is slightly longer than the stamens, so favouring cross-pollination, which is usually achieved by bumble bees.

True lilies belong to the genus *Lilium* and there are about one hundred north temperate species of which the Turk's Cap Lily is an example. Many other flowers in the family are also known as lilies however. Well-known members of the family not already mentioned include asparagus, tulips, dog's-tooth violets or adder's tongues and butcher's broom.

The Iris family is composed of plants with flat sword-like or grass-like leaves with showy flowers whose parts are arranged in threes. As with some lilies, sometimes the sepals and petals look alike so that the flowers appear to have six petals. The word Iris is the Greek for rainbow, and there are indeed a variety of colours to be found in these flowers. Iris flowers are frequently multi-coloured as are these mauve ones tinged with yellow and white shown growing in a meadow near Lake Constance *left*. Gladioli, like Irises, are familiar garden flowers but there are about one hundred and fifty species to be found growing wild in Europe, the Mediterranean and Africa. This delicate red flower *right* is McKinder's Gladiolus and was photographed on Mount Kenya.

Crocuses (genus *Crocus) below* are also native to the Mediterranean. Saffron, used as a dye and for flavouring, comes from the stigmas of the Saffron *Crocus sativus;* this should not be confused with the Meadow Saffron (page 50) which belongs to another family and is poisonous.

The Daffodil or Amaryllis family is another family of bulbed plants with grass-like leaves. The flowers again are showy and often lily-like. Two contrasting members are shown here, the Blood-flower or Fireball Lily from tropical Africa *left* and delicate Snowdrops *below* which appear in spring in Europe.

Several species of Fireball Lily flower more profusely after fires and some have the ability to lie dormant for many years, flowering when the conditions become favourable. A new species was discovered in 1961 when a normally marshy area was burnt after an unusually long drought. Four or five days after the fire the brilliant red flower buds appeared—the bulbs must have been dormant for decades.

Yuccas are native to tropical America and range from tiny shrubs to trees over fifteen metres tall. Their leaves grow in dense clusters and normally have horny edges and spiny tips. The Soaptree Yucca is illustrated here *above.* The flowers are white; they open and emit a sweet scent at night which attracts the female Yucca moth. All species of Yucca east of the Rockies are pollinated by this one kind of moth. She does not come to the flower to feed but to lay her eggs which she deposits in the ovary. Then she deliberately pushes pollen, usually collected from the stamens of another plant, down on to the stigmas. The plant comes to no harm because many other ovules besides those that she has parasitised develop into seeds.

The succulent Agaves or Century Plants come from the same part of the world as the Yuccas and are closely related to them. *Agave scabra, right* , is found in the southwestern United States and north Mexico. Many species flower once only and then die, but they have an unusually long life-cycle; the flowers do not appear until the plant has been growing for thirty years or so. Some species are reputed not to flower until the plant is one hundred years old.

Estimates of the number of species in the Orchid family vary wildly from five to thirty-five thousand; however it is generally agreed that the family is a large one. The majority of species are tropical or subtropical epiphytes growing on the branches and trunks of trees. The temperate Orchids are all terrestrial plants and are noted for growing in intimate association with fungi, which grow in or closely applied to their roots, without which many of them cannot survive.

The Purple Enamel Orchid *top left* is a native to Western Australia where it is common and widespread. It is another plant, that, despite many efforts to do so, has resisted all attempts to introduce it into gardens. This must be because all the necessary conditions for its growth are not satisfied in such surroundings, and this could well be because of the absence of its fungal partner. The flower structure of the Orchids is the most specialised in all the plant kingdom. Many rely on one insect species alone to pollinate them often attracting these insects by scent. Some orchids even produce different scents at different times. There is a species of *Dendrobium* which smells of heliotrope in the morning and lilac at night. A species of *Dendrobium* growing in New Guinea is shown *below left*.

Orchids of the genus *Angraecum* produce nectar in very long tubular spurs. There is a species in Madagascar, *A. sesquipedale*, which has spurs up to thirty centimetres long but the nectar collects only in the last four centimetres. A species of moth with a correspondingly long proboscis which can reach the nectar pollinates the flowers. *Angraecum germinyanum, right,* was photographed in Grand Comoré in the Indian Ocean.

The European Orchids of the genus *Ophrys* are well-known for the striking resemblance of their flowers to various insects. They are unique in that the reward that they offer to their pollinators is not food but, by scent, shape, colour and touch, they deceive male insects into believing that a willing female awaits to mate with them. The insect thus assumes a position suitable for inadvertently collecting the pollen, which, as in most Orchids, is arranged in two masses bound together by elastic threads and known as pollinia. These are sticky and attach themselves to the insect, usually to its head. After about half a minute, as the pollinia dry out, they swing through an angle of about 90° and so become perfectly placed to attach to the stigmas when the insect visits another flower.

The British Bee Orchid *over page* is an *Ophrys* species which shows a further evolutionary step; it has lost its bee pollinator and is now, following modification of the anther cells, nearly always self-pollinated.

GLOSSARY

Annual, a plant which completes its life cycle (including death) in a single season.

Anther, the terminal part of the stamen containing pollen.

Bract, a small relatively undeveloped leaf which bears a flower in the angle between it and the stem.

Calyx, the outermost part of many flowers consisting of leaf-like sepals.

Corolla, the conspicuous part of the flower within the calyx consisting of a number of petals.

Cross-pollination, transfer of pollen from one flower to the stigma of another flower of another plant of the same species.

Disc floret, a central fertile member of the typical composite inflorescence.

Epiphyte, a plant growing on another plant using it solely as support.

Family, a group used in classifying plants (and other organisms) consisting of a number of genera.

Floret, a small flower.

Genus (plural **genera**), a group used in classifying organisms of lower rank than a family and consisting of closely related species

Habitat, a natural place of growth; the physical environment of a community.

Herb, a plant with no woody and persistent stem above the ground.

Hybrid, a plant resulting from a cross between two genetically dissimilar parents.

Inflorescence, a flowering shoot, aggregation of a number of flowers on an axis.

Involucre, a ring of bracts around an inflorescence (as in a daisy).

Ovary, the part of the flower that contains the ovules which, after fertilisation, give rise to the seeds.

Perennial, a plant which lives for more than two years and usually flowers each year.

Perianth, the modified leaves that form the outer part of the flower, i.e. calyx and corolla if these are present.

Petal, a modified leaf forming part of the corolla.

Photosynthesis, the process by which green plants make carbohydrates from water and carbon dioxide (sunlight and the green pigment chlorophyll are both essential).

Pistil, the ovary of a flower with its style and stigma.

Pollination, the transfer of pollen from anther to stigma.

Ray floret, marginal, infertile member of the typical composite inflorescence.

Self-pollination, the transfer of pollen from the anther to stigma of the same flower or to the stigma of another flower on the same plant.

Sepal, one of the usually green and leaf-like parts forming the calyx in many flowers.

Shrub, a low woody plant.

Spadix (plural **spadices**), a spike of flowers borne on a fleshy stalk.

Spathe, a large bract that envelops certain kinds of inflorescence, especially spadices.

Species, a group of closely-allied mutually fertile individuals–the smallest unit of classification normally used.

Stamen, the pollen producing part of the flower consisting of anther and filament.

Stigma, the terminal expansion of the style surface which receives the pollen.

Style, the slender prolongation of the ovary of the plant which bears the stigma.

Succulent, a plant that stores water in its tissues giving a fleshy appearance and enabling it to withstand drought.

Symbiosis, an association of dissimilar organisms to their mutual advantage.

Vine, a climbing or trailing stem.

First published in Great Britain 1978 by Colour Library International Ltd.
Designed by David Gibbon. Produced by Ted Smart.
© Text: Jacqueline Seymour © Illustrations: CLI/Bruce Coleman Ltd.
Colour separations by La Cromolito, Milan, Italy.
Display and Text filmsetting by Focus Photoset, London, England.
Printed and bound by L.E.G.O. Vicenza, Italy.
All rights reserved.
ISBN No. 0 904681 40 8
COLOUR LIBRARY INTERNATIONAL

INDEX